WHEN THE TRUST
BREAKS

WHEN THE TRUST
BREAKS

Healing Psychological, Spiritual, *and* Emotional Wounds

JAMES GRETEMAN, C.S.C.

Paulist Press
New York/Mahwah, N.J.

Cover design by Trudi Gershenov
Book design by Lynn Else

Library of Congress Cataloging-in-Publication Data

Greteman, Jim.
  When the trust breaks : healing psychological, spiritual, *and* emotional wounds / James Greteman.
     p. cm.
  Includes bibliographical references.
  ISBN 0-8091-4149-3 (alk. paper)
  1. Mental health—Religious aspects—Christianity. 2. Imagination—Religious aspects—Christianity. I. Title.
  BT732.4 G74 2003
  248.8′62—dc21

                                                          2003004243

Published by Paulist Press
997 Macarthur Boulevard
Mahwah, New Jersey 07430

www.paulistpress.com

Printed and bound in the United States of America

Contents

Acknowledgments

This book came about from my experiences working with hurting people over the past forty years. Besides wanting to thank them, there are others to thank who helped to influence what I am writing. There is my religious community, Congregation of Holy Cross, in Indiana, that has done so much for me. There is also my family in Iowa that has given me love and understanding. There are my professional colleagues in various parts of the country, and there are special friends, one could say mentors, Joseph Parrinello and Leon Haverkamp, who made this book better by their wisdom and gentle guidance. I also thank Christine Jensen Hogan who got all the pronouns, sentences and paragraphs in the right places. Any deficiencies are entirely my own. I also want to thank the publishing professionals who make this book a reality.

Introduction

Why this book? Because, after working with people the past forty years doing therapy, giving workshops, and teaching, I have come to the conclusion that many people have serious, unresolved hurts from earlier in life. These hurts take much of our present energy to hold them down, and therefore influence our present behavior by our not being able to focus our total energy on the present situation.

What are some of the hurts I've heard people describe from their early life? Here are some examples: their parents abused them over and over when they were young, saying they were worthless; parents, other adults, brothers or sisters abused them sexually; marriage partners or friends put them down to their face, sometimes in front of a group, with very cutting remarks; certain people used humor in a cruel way at their expense, to make themselves look good. There are many other examples that could be added to this list. The difficulty with such experiences is that they are remembered, and much of our present behavior is filtered through these hurts. So sometimes we just do not trust, or do not risk growth in our present situation.

After working with and listening to people over a period of forty years, I have come up with a gentle process that seems to help people let go of old hurts and heal from these past experiences.

This process is based on thinking in a new way, using the imagination and intuition to gently help to bring about change. This is not magic, but shows how to use the subconscious mind to help make a change. It is estimated that we only use about three percent of our brain, which is the conscious area. What if we could activate part of the unconscious by using the imagination to help us heal that part of us which is broken? This is what we will do, using this book.

If this process does not work for you, talk to a professional counselor about your situation; but whichever way you try to heal from it, go gently. It is not necessary to add more hurts to the old hurts. Hurts add up.

The Stories

The six stories I am about to relate are true. They are about people I have worked with over the years in various of these United States. The names I have used, of course, are fictitious. Each story has a beginning, a middle, and an end. The beginning is where each of these persons got hurt, and the middle is how each of them carried that hurt on and on. It is the same with our own stories. If we hold on to our hurts, the end is not very healthy for any of us. By looking at the stories of these six people, each of us can discover something about the process of healing our own primal hurt.

Sally

Sally is now fifty-four years old and tells the following story. When she was growing up, the fourth child in a family of six, her brothers and sisters were always more assertive. The result was that she never got her needs met and soon started to take this for granted. When she was in high school some of the students would pick on her. One boy was extremely mean and would say things about her clothes, since her family could not always buy the latest fashions. Sally kept these hurts to herself, but they started to add up. After high school, Sally worked for several years, dated a few times—

mostly people she did not like—and then met Bill. Bill had a nice side to him and they finally decided to get married. Later, after several children, stress came into the marriage because Sally could not work and Bill did not make enough money to support the family. In his frustration, he started to pick on Sally. To Sally it was like reopening an old wound, one that still hurt. Twenty-seven years later, Sally sought counseling, saying she was not happy with herself, her husband, and her present situation, and felt trapped.

Sam

Sam came into my office when he was thirty-eight years old. He had a far-away look in his eyes and said that he had to do something. Sam was recently divorced from his second wife and was fighting with everyone. After some tears, Sam told me his story. He grew up with his younger brother in a family where his father was in the military. His father was a large man who was abusive and alcoholic. His mother was never there. Sam told a story of his father coming home drunk most weekends and trying to use his younger brother sexually. Since the bed was up against the wall, Sam had protected his younger brother by offering his body instead. This went on until he was sixteen, when he was large enough to beat his father with a bat. The court put him in the military instead of in jail. A year later, while he was serving in the military, his friends got him drunk and he told his story. After that, some of the squad abused him, and again he used a bat. After getting out of the military on a dishonorable discharge, he experienced several failed marriages. Sam felt that he could not maintain a successful relationship because of what was inside of him.

Alice

Alice was a bright little girl in the third grade. One day her class was having a spelling contest. She told me that she always got a hundred in spelling. She was asked to spell egg in the second round of the contest and, not paying close enough attention, spelled it a-g-g. The teacher, who was not having a good day, put her down for three or four minutes before the class. Alice felt destroyed. After this she always believed she was a poor speller, and years later, when something didn't go right in high school, college, or even in later life, Alice again felt that she was no good. She even kept a record of all the things that she thought she was doing wrong. When I began to see her she was sixty-one years old!

John

John was seventeen when his adoptive parents brought him in for counseling. He was fighting with his sisters most of the time. John said that he got mostly A's in school, but just did not care. After seeing him for five months, I felt that I was getting nowhere and his parents agreed. However, John had heard that I do hypnosis, and asked if I would hypnotize him in order to help him find out what was wrong.

His parents gave their assent, so we did one session. In that session, John exhibited a lot of energy around the subject of his adoption process, so we replayed what happened during that time. John explained that it was snowing very hard outside, and that the nurse who was holding him (he was three) was very angry because the adoptive parents were late getting there. John stated that the nurse said several times, "I wish they would get here, since you're just a throwaway baby anyway!" John remembers this vividly in his unconscious.

Mary

When I first saw Mary, at age twenty-three, she was sitting in my office looking very unhappy. She said that her finances were a mess, along with her relationships. Her car was always breaking down, and she owed everyone, but just kept on spending money. Mary said that she grew up in a fairly normal family, but that her mother was unhappy because her husband was never home, and because she often spent money they did not have. The mother took her frustrations out on Mary, telling her that she was just like her father, since the father favored Mary.

Hank

Hank was very old and was dying, but for some reason he would not let go. After talking with me for about fifteen sessions, he finally revealed the secret of his hurt. He told about being abused when he was ten, and how his uncle had said that he, Hank, had caused it. He had carried this hurt for over eighty-five years!

What about *your* hurt? How many years have you carried it around? In the next chapter we will look at how to build some emotional energy so that we can begin to deal with this primal hurt.

The Energy Source

There are a number of reasons why we have carried our hurt around with us for years. One is based on our energy source, which for many of us was very low or non-existent. When people came into my office for counseling, I asked them how they got there. Most said they came by car or truck. I would then ask them: "What does the car run on?" When they replied "Gas," I asked them what *they* ran on. They would say things like food, or prayer, or something else.

Then I would explain that they carried psychic energy as a kind of fuel in their system. If their tank of psychic energy was empty, they would have little to run on. Let me elaborate. If you've spent all day making a large pot of chili for friends coming over after a football game, you've had to work on the ingredients and the seasonings. When they come, you give some to this one and that one, and finally the whole group. Then you discover there is none left for you. Like most of us, you have been trained to give but not to take. But there is a part of you that feels angry. If you give and give, there will be nothing left in your energy tank. There is nothing wrong in giving, but all of us need time to refill our energy source. What if we could do this without hurting others or being self-ish? The following is a short technique for doing this.

When Alice came into my office the second time, I asked her what shoe she puts on first in the morning, the right one or the left. She stated that she did not know. I explained that about eighty percent of the people do not know which shoe they put on first, because it is a habit they do without thinking. She could build a new habit in her mind by setting up a new pattern, giving herself positive reinforcement, known also as "stroking." Using stroking she could exchange a negative pattern for a positive one. Together we looked for patterns of positive reinforcement that would work for her. Each time Alice would look in the mirror, she would tell herself how pretty her eyes were. She would make a conscious decision to do this regardless of how she was actually feeling. Anytime she did something around the house she would tell herself that she did a good job. She would do this five or six times a day. Anyone who does this, usually within two weeks can sense a difference in how they feel. After six weeks it gets to be a habit, like putting on your shoes. So Alice learned to build positive energy in herself which strengthened her to make needed changes.

Each of us needs to build a positive energy source so we have something in our tank to handle everyday situations, especially when we run into a primal hurt. In some places this is called self-affirmation. It helps us feel better about ourselves. No, you won't get the bighead or be selfish. This is a very healthy exercise. This does not make you conceited, nor will it hurt others, for it is a completely mental exercise.

Sometimes it is a good idea to write down each day five or six things you feel you did well—to give yourself positive strokes. For example:

1. I did a good job doing the laundry today (remember to count things like this).

The Traps

So what happens, you might ask, when these people fill up with psychic energy, but still fail to move past their primal hurt? Not much. They are stuck. To move forward, they have to start forgiving. Sally would say to me, "I don't feel like forgiving him." Forgiveness is a mental decision and not a feeling. This decision is usually made in small parts, and is not based on feelings. It's similar to coming up to a wall, touching it, and pulling back. The result is that you never get over the wall and move on in life. You're trapped. Before discussing what forgiveness is, let's look at some of the traps that Hank, Alice, and the others fell into.

Many of the people that I work with confuse this point and think that forgiveness is the same as excusing. No, Hank does not have to excuse the person that abused him. But by mixing these two concepts, Hank carried his secret for seventy-five years. Just think of the amount of psychic energy Hank had to use to keep this primal hurt down, and the amount of suffering that he went through! Maybe you also have confused forgiveness with excusing. Part of our humanness is that we do not always have all the correct tools to handle every decision. If you got caught in a place of being unforgiving, it is very important that you be gentle with yourself.

We can also confuse forgiveness with reconciling. Sam would express very strong feelings about his father, who was still an alcoholic and in prison. He felt that if he saw his father, he would kill him for what he had done to his younger brother and to him. When Sam thought about it, he could never see himself reconciling with his father. Maybe that was not even possible until the father made some changes. But by mixing this concept of reconciliation with forgiveness, Sam kept himself in jail. Each time he came up to the wall or bars, he would pull back and stay angry and hurt. If Sam could start to forgive, he could move on with his life.

Mary confused forgiveness with forgetting. Mary will always have a sad memory about what her mother said to her. But if she chooses to forgive, it will remain only a sad memory, and Mary can move on in life. She may have to work on the pattern that she uses with new situations, and develop new coping mechanisms that are not colored by what her mother said about her. She can substitute a more positive or healthy pattern for the one that her mother taught her.

John had a fourth pattern, identifying forgiveness with weakness. He stated that internally he always felt that he was not okay since he was just a throwaway baby. This he never shared with anyone. Just think of the level of hurt he carried in his young life, which he could not talk about. This was so deep in his unconscious that it would only come up to scare him when he was half asleep. In reality, John was a very good student and above average in sports. His behavior was bad at home and at school, which confirmed his self-image of being just a throwaway baby. His actions were an expression of his feelings of anger.

When people confuse forgiveness with excusing, reconciling, forgetting, or weakness, they keep themselves locked behind a wall. Everyone who does this will follow the same pattern.

Take some time to quiet yourself and very slowly look at the patterns or traps that you might have set up. First, consider awareness. For when you become aware you have a choice: to change or not to change. If you stay unaware, the pattern or trap just continues. Don't get restless or discouraged with yourself. One person I worked with became aware of her continuing pattern and would mentally say "Stop." Then she would ask God to handle the problem, if she could not. Maybe you could set up some gentle ways to help yourself. Make a list of them here.

1.

2.

3.

The next chapter will add more suggestions for helping you to replace unhealthy patterns of behavior.

A Fantasy

It sounds as if like we are going to have to make a change if we are going to let go of this primal hurt. Many of us have tried to lose weight, stop smoking, or rid ourselves of some other habit that is bothering us. But change is difficult, especially in relation to a primal hurt because of fear, or some other reason. So let's try a different technique, one that is gentle but still helps us to change. I once heard a speaker say that we only use three percent of our brain. This person also said that if we used fifty percent of our brain, we could learn six or seven languages and memorize a dictionary in six months. So we are going to use more of the brain, the imagination, to cross over to the unconscious in order to plant some seeds of change.

Sit in a comfortable chair where you can put your feet up. Lie back in the chair and do not cross your legs or arms, for in starting this relaxation we will slow the circulation down and anything crossed tends to fall asleep. Open your mouth about a quarter of an inch, and take a normal breath of air; hold it a second and slowly blow it out through your mouth. After slowly blowing it out, pull in the stomach so that all the air goes out. Do this four or five times to establish a nice slow pattern. The body will slowly relax. You may ask, What if I fall asleep? No harm done, for you will wake up after sleeping awhile. Some people like to close their eyes, for thirty percent of your energy flows out through your eyes. Then imagine that your head slowly relaxes and any tightness is released when you slowly breathe out. Do this with each part of the body: the neck, shoulders, upper arms, lower arms, the chest, stomach, hips, knees, calves, ankles, and feet. Take your time, for this will totally relax your body, and make the area between consciousness and unconsciousness less solid and more yielding. When this happens it is very easy to plant a suggestion about yourself that leads to change.

Imagine being in some natural setting by yourself, where you feel extremely comfortable. Let your senses slowly tune into nature in this special place. Listen carefully. You may be able to hear birds, the rustle of leaves, or the sound of water. What scents can you pick up? In your imagination, what do you see or feel? Maybe a soft breath of air, or the sunshine on your face and entire body. Some will say that they don't sense anything, while others will notice one or more items. As you're sitting, let your body tune into nature, for the rhythms of nature heal.

Then, using your imagination, plant one idea over and over, slowly repeating this statement. "I am slowly letting go of this hurt and I'm healing." Make it simple and positive. If you believe in God, add to the statement "God is perfect health." Research has shown that a universal force helps with healing. If you get anxious when doing this, it is okay to return in your imagination to the safe place in nature. After doing this for a short time, slowly open your eyes and sit comfortably in the chair. Do not hop up for the telephone or doorbell—you may fall down since your circulation has slowed down. If you do decide to answer such a call, how-ever, slowly move your hands and feet first, and then care-fully get up. Do not do this exercise in the car, or you may cause an accident.

My idea that I repeat over and over is...

Forgiveness

Why do we human beings hurt each other so often? This group against that group, that group against this group; and if we can get enough people together, a war by this country against that country. Mike McCullough, author of *To Forgive Is Human*, uses this Chinese proverb: "The person who seeks revenge should dig two graves." McCullough explains that if people nurture revenge or anger about a previous hurt, they are more vulnerable to an increased heart rate and high blood pressure, which can cause heart disease. In some of his studies, he has concluded that the persons who forgive those who harmed them—even six weeks after they have been hurt—are less depressed or anxious, sleep better, and are free of obsessive thoughts and revenge fantasies. Robert Enright, from the University of Wisconsin at Madison, stated in his research that if people would forgive those who deeply hurt them, they would heal emotionally.

So what is this concept of forgiveness? It's difficult to give a definition of forgiveness because it is partly spiritual and abstract. Enright says that forgiveness is like giving up the resentment to which you are entitled and developing a friendlier attitude to the person that hurt you, even though that person is not entitled to this. After working with people for some forty years, I have come to the conclusion that forgiveness is a decision and not a feeling. There is some self-sacrifice involved. But it is also to benefit yourself that you forgive, as this helps you heal. You usually do this in a series of small steps, something like going up the stairs to the second floor. It does not mean that that you endorse what the person did to you. Reaching the place of forgiveness takes time and it is important that you not give up. For instance, you may say to God, "I can't handle it anymore," and turn it over to God. This would mean letting go, which you might have to do a number of times. A person in one of my groups used to say, "God, you created this person and I'm giving him back." Over a period of a year her anger diminished and she did let go. A book by a Trappist monk, William A. Meninger, entitled *The Process of Forgiveness,* tells how forgiveness is related to wholeness. He recounts how an angry person attracts angry people around him, or an unfriendly person gravitates toward people who respond in an unfriendly way.

As I read about the people that were in the camps in the various wars, I noticed that those who survived in the best condition were the ones who forgave their captors. Maybe we could start a new revolution: if we forgive the persons that hurt us, then maybe families would start to forgive other families, and finally nations would forgive other nations. Robert Enright tells us that South Africa, with the efforts by Desmund TuTu, Nelson Mandela, and others toward forgiving those who practiced apartheid, gives us a good example of this.

But mixed in with this concept of forgiveness is a surface emotion that blocks many of us from changing, and that emotion is *anger*. We have difficulty getting past our anger to get to the deeper hurt and then to forgiveness.

Try this exercise:

Quiet yourself and relax your body. Ask yourself what seems to be blocking your progress. Are you getting energy from staying angry? What blocks are you putting in the way of a healthier you?

Anger

Some of the people I worked with would tell me time after time that they didn't want to be angry. Anger is a normal emotion which most of us use to distance ourselves from someone or something that may have hurt us. But why did anger become a problem for Hank, Sally, Sam, and the others? If it is a normal response to being abused, then how could it be a problem? They could not express this anger properly, so the anger was either frozen or internalized. Moreover, if they expressed it, they were likely to be subjected to more abuse. Some were also caught in further emotions, like guilt or shame.

So what would be some healthy ways of getting this anger out? Sam's anger was like a dam, and his fear was that if he let it out, he would cause destruction to himself or someone else. The technique that helped Sam was getting very relaxed in a chair and visualizing his anger as gray smoke. Each time he breathed out he imagined blowing out some of the smoke. Over a period of time his anger lessened.

Sally was my writer. Each week she would get out her notebook and journal, and write down her feelings about the situation. Over a period of four months the emotion diminished, as though she had shaken a bottle of pop and let the fizz out. This is a very safe method for lowering the energy level of an emotion. One thing that we must remember is that we may have to give up a relationship in which there is continual strife, or one in which there is any kind of abuse. Each situation involving anger is different.

Some people like to talk their anger out with a friend. But this takes time and may put a lot of stress on a friendship. A good counselor can help. Friends tend to run out of patience after they have heard the story once. I like to get the person very relaxed and then have him or her imagine taking a child's vacuum cleaner to vacuum out the parts in the mind that contain this hurt. Afterward, most are left with just a sad memory of the situation.

If a picture is worth a thousand words to you, then get relaxed in a chair, picture a large clear screen in front of you, and then project the situation onto this screen. Then imagine you have a broom and that you are slowly sweeping the picture from the screen.

By using the imagination we can all change, since ninety-seven percent of the brain is in the subconscious. When you imagine, things start to change. If you add your power from God, change happens faster. I encourage you to try some of these safe techniques to deal with your anger. There are many books available on this subject. One I like is *The Dance of Anger*, by Harriet Goldhor Lerner.

Another variation involves the use of color with the imagination. Sit in a comfortable chair to do the following exercise, with your feet flat on the floor (or at least not crossed), and your arms resting on the chair by your side. Slowly inhale through your nose and breathe out through your mouth. As you inhale, picture a white light coming into your lungs, and as you exhale picture a dirty color passing out through the mouth. As you continue, you will picture the lungs getting whiter and whiter until they glow with whiteness. When you do this, the anger can get less and less and the lungs heal. Other organs can have other colors: the kidneys can be light blue, the liver light green, the heart light red, and the spleen pale yellow. Each time you exhale, a darker color leaves and the anger in that organ becomes less.

The meditation is based on the archetypal and primordial forces in our bodies. It should always be done in a gentle way. After a short time, stop. This meditation can be repeated many times. As you imagine the anger getting less and less, change will happen.

Beyond Anger

After getting past the surface of the wound, which in this situation is the anger, you move to the next level of the hurt. This, for the people I worked with, was the pain of the hurt itself. Just what is that pain? Pain signals to you that something is wrong, and this happens on several different levels.

One level that shows up very quickly with the hurt is the physical level. This pain could be rated from one to ten; you would determine whether it was a one, with only slight pain, or a ten, which you could not stand. Each of us has a different limit to what we can stand. Some can take a lot; while others cannot handle very much. Most people wait too long before asking for help. Some hurting people, like Sam, tend to self medicate. Sam took all kinds of pills from the pharmacy, and eventually took illicit drugs to help alleviate the pain. Besides pills, people look at alternative methods of medicine to help with pain. Most of these are noninvasive methods, such as hypnosis.

Another level of pain is the emotional level, which for most of us is quite complicated. Sam was very angry all the time; Sally was always sad; Mary felt a lot of anxiety; John felt grief most of the time; and Hank was in terror as he aged. In the case of physical pain, if your foot hurts, you go to the foot doctor. With emotional pain, it is not as clear what to do. All of us experience painful emotions at some time in our life. These emotions are normal, but if they are experienced for up to a year or more, then it is time to get help.

Why didn't Hank or Alice seek help sooner for their situations? Some of us become attached to the pain. It can be easier to face the pain than the risk involved with any change. One person I worked with had a very painful divorce and could tell me how many years, months, days, and hours she had been divorced. Her identity was no longer in her name, but in the fact that she was divorced.

Each of these people was confused about pain. They believed that emotional pain was not real pain; it was not like physical pain, which they understood and could fix fairly simply and quickly with a phone call or trip to the doctor. Emotional pain can't be fixed quickly or simply. As a result, this emotional pain was impairing their ability to make healthy decisions about their lives. Most felt that there was something wrong, but they continued to make poor decisions or none at all. One sure sign that they were trapped was the fact that they felt depressed. Mary always believed that she had a role to play, to be like her father. Sam escaped into fantasy, so that the pain of what his father did to him was not so great. Sally spent most of her time in a dream world rather than face the reality of her troubled marriage. A sign of their depression was the way they would strike out in anger when there was no reason.

Think of small children when they get angry. Some pout or cry to show their feelings, or even throw a tantrum, but as adults we are many times in a strong mood. Not all of these adults stay in counseling because many want an instant answer—like magic. Even in hypnosis some want magic by saying, "I will give you one try to fix me." My reply is that we can fix clocks, cars, and other such things fairly quickly, while caring for and healing of emotional hurts takes longer. Besides physical and emotional pain, there is an inner loneliness, a longing for wholeness, a longing for God. M. Scott Peck describes this as existential pain, facing and dealing with life's problems. Just as all of us have families that are not perfect, or people that we work with who can be difficult at times, so too we have to learn what pain we are responsible for and what pain we are not responsible for in life.

So if we are looking for solutions for our pain, we must realize that sometimes there are solutions, but other times there are not. If you are not sure which is the case with your pain, please talk it over with someone who cares. God did not put you here just to suffer.

What Part Does Tension Play?

Your hurt, when expressed in the form of pain, makes you draw back. So does tension. When you are hurt physically, say by touching a hot stove, you pull back. When you are hurt mentally, you do the same thing. With a primal hurt you also pull back, but the tendency is to stay that way, as if you have locked yourself in jail. If you take your hand and make a tight fist, you feel tension. When you let go and open the hand you can feel it beginning to relax. All of us send one signal at a time to the hand—either to tense up or relax. This is normal. In primal hurts the tendency is to keep the hand in a tight fist. This can cause a lot of pain or tension if maintained over some time. Imagine what can happen to our entire body if we are stressed out for a long period of time.

One of the first symptoms of tension is isolation. We pull back from our friends and family, and later from institutions, such as church. We think that other people don't want to hear our problem, or we are nervous about sharing our story. The tension increases because these people were not there with positive support when our primal hurt occurred. Moving physically from the place where the situation happened, or building emotional walls around ourselves, increases this isolation. Some of us, like Hank, have the fantasy that living a life of a hermit will make things better. Most of us choose, when we are hurting, to live behind a closed door.

Another symptom of tension is rage. Sam always found himself striking out at those closest to him. He found this wasn't acceptable, so he internalized his rage and found himself breaking inanimate objects. Many times when he came in to see me he would have bruises or cuts on his hands. He said that he felt like a time bomb some of the time. Alice would manifest her tensions by blaming all men for her discontent. As she continued to count the wrongs of others, Alice found it difficult to keep a job and fought with her peers at work.

Sam dealt with his tension by avoiding his feelings, so that he came across as being very cold and unfeeling. In his relationships, he had trouble showing love and caring to his partner. To do this he would have had to thaw out his own feelings. His fear was that if he did this, he would not be able to stop crying, or that he would go crazy.

Another symptom with all of them was guilt—thinking that they were somehow responsible for this primal hurt. Sally had sleep disturbances and nightmares. This was true for many of the people that came to see me, taking the form of recurrent dreams. Talking to someone about the dream, or even journaling—getting a notebook and writing down the dream—helps take some of the energy out of the dream. It is important not to judge yourself about the content of your dreams. Dreams cannot hurt you. In the next chapter we will look at some ways to help decrease stress.

Releasing the Stress

Stress affected the physical, emotional, and spiritual lives of the people in our six stories. Each needed to lower his or her stress level. It would be similar to blowing up a balloon and having too much pressure in the balloon. Each time you let some air out of the balloon, there would be less pressure. There are some areas where one can relieve stress and thereby reduce the pressure.

One area is the physical body. The body needs to be taken care of as much as our well-being. Overeating, or eating too much sugar or junk food, does damage to the body. I would ask the persons I was working with if they were eating one or two pieces of fresh fruit each day. I asked how much exercise they had over the past week. Walking can do wonders to help the body regulate itself. Alice agreed that she would try to take a nature walk someplace four times a week, for twenty to thirty minutes each time. Nature has a beautiful way of helping the body regulate itself. The patterns of nature are mostly calm, and this seems to pass on to the body. Gentle steps toward eating well and exercising daily help to let some of the air out of the balloon of stress.

Calming the mind is another way of letting go of stress. Just sitting down for twenty minutes in a quiet place can help. Slowly take a look at what your stress points are and what really sets you off. After reflecting for five minutes, take one of the stresses and imagine placing it in a basket tied to a weather balloon. Now, as you slowly breathe in through the nose and out through the mouth, watch the basket with the balloon gradually rise and drift away. Sally liked to do this exercise. After a period of time, Sally noticed that she still had her problem, but that certain elements of it did not bother her as much, especially resentment.

Sam had to look at certain places near where he lived that always bothered him. When he went to gun shows, he was usually irritated the next day. Since he liked gun shows, he would always allow some private space the following day to process what was going on within himself.

John noticed that he was touchy whenever others talked about adoption. He would have to reaffirm that he was okay and was not just a throwaway baby without value. Sam had to watch physical spaces while John's were more mental. You may also have to look closely at certain areas of the environment that help your own balloon get larger.

Just as each person had to look at his or her physical, mental, and environmental areas of stress, Hank had to look at some spiritual areas that bothered him. Hank had to talk to someone regarding the guilt he was feeling about what had happened when he was very small. He came to realize that this guilt was unrealistic and had to be let go of, along with the fear he had built up over the years.

All the persons I worked with had to look at their stress and find ways to lower the pressure in their balloon. To lift their mood some walked, some took time to smell the flowers, or put a pleasant note on the refrigerator, or work in the garden. Some watched a funny show on TV, called a friend, said a prayer, or did something else that helped them. You can do similar things that can change your attitude or help you grow in the direction that can help you to proceed. I once read that we either grow or die; we don't stand still. The choice is personal.

Stress continued to be a problem for Sally and she always felt there was too much to do. This caused her to worry that she was not pleasing all the people around her. This showed itself often in the form of a queasy stomach. Hank, on the other hand, experienced his stress by often feeling tired because of an inner restlessness that he could not overcome. John noticed that when his stress level was high, he would feel overly excited. We talked about the fact that some stress is normal, since it is okay not to be perfect. As these people learned to relax by using their own methods of letting go, their levels of stress became more manageable. Even talking to a friend sometimes helped them to lower their stress and feel better.

Some of their family members would habitually unload *their* problems on them, adding to their already overstressed lives. One technique we used for healing with this was to put up an imaginary umbrella and let those problems run off of it like rain, and not add them to their own stresses. As they did this, they felt more and more at ease. They began to experience more freedom and much more joy in their lives.

Understanding Imagery

Each of the people I have been writing about had problems which produced too much clutter in their minds. Each had to create a safe space with boundaries and structures within which change could take place. Then they could enter this safe place to experience new ways of valuing themselves or to give themselves a healthy message. All found some situation in their life that created problems for themselves, just as you may experience something that needs healing. Using the imagination in this safe place allowed them, as it will allow you, to deal with a hurtful or confusing situation—their primal hurt. Just as their hurt did not take place in a vacuum, neither did yours. So we all need a safe and private place to start. Then we need to step out of this safe place and to experience others.

But why use imaging? Sometimes we need to use another state of consciousness so that we can see things from a new perspective. When we were children we all had an imagination, but for many of us that healthy part of ourselves was not developed. Our imagination can be an agent of change. It can help us to stretch our reality. By use of our imagination we can build a bridge between our unconscious and our conscious world. As a child, you may have had a special chair, or a window looking out into the yard, where you sat, looked, and imagined something. We are going to look at the process of imaging so that we can bring that richness and color back into our lives. Visualizing images not only uses our sense of sight, but all our senses. Remembering those special smells from the kitchen, or while walking in the woods in the spring, may bring an image to your mind.

The people I worked with used several types of imagery. One was the type which occurs when you are falling asleep or just waking up. You can experience this type of imagery by relaxing in a chair, taking several deep breaths, and watching what happens. You might experience a pain in your back, or some other message from your body. Just be open to those signals as you observe them. One can enter this imagery in another way by becoming active with it. Imagine some warm water slowly running over this area of discomfort. Your body will respond more quickly to an image than it will to words. Mary always had difficulty falling asleep in the evening. She would get angry with herself when, after telling herself to fall asleep, nothing happened. I suggested that she picture herself on a beach watching the waves slowly coming in to the shore. If you could go into a store and shop for a kind of image, what kind would you pick? It could be the type mentioned in the previous paragraph—the image that just comes to you from a certain smell—may enter into that image. Another would be going back to a particular behavior that happened to you when you were younger, and replaying the situation in a more acceptable manner. Some of the people I worked with would even add a lot of humor to the situation. They would do this by creating an imaginary window through which they could observe the past. Behind this window they felt safe and in control of the situation.

John, in response to the pain he felt over his adoption, reimagined what happened so that the nurse remarked what a beautiful little boy he was and danced around the room while holding him. He told me that he could feel the happiness she felt. He imagined his new family arriving, and witnessed the intense joy that they felt being able to adopt such a fine young man. He pictured them placing him in the new car seat and savored the happiness he felt in the car as they left for his new home. Then came the excitement of arriving at his new home and meeting all the new relatives and friends, of being held by different people who were all so happy to see him, and finally, of being put to bed by two loving parents who gently put the comforter around him. This is another type of imagery which pictures what you wanted the final result to be, and the process that you took to get there. Whenever you go upstairs, there are a number of steps you have to take. Imagine each step as a step to your goal, and try to fill in details that help you get those steps taken care of in a healthy way.

Another image that Hank used was this: He pictured himself with God and with everything between them as being okay. I, many times, imagine myself to be a flower in a garden. I can stand alone and be the type of flower I want to be, and yet still belong to the garden and have the support of the other flowers around me. If you choose to picture yourself as a flower, what type of flower would you like to be?

Next, we are going to do some exercises that can be used or adapted to your own specific needs.

My Own Image

Building an image for change in this process has three parts: a beginning, a middle, and an end. The beginning is a time of relaxation, which can be short or long depending on the depth at which you want to plant the idea. The middle is where the image is planted after you have relaxed your body. This can be long or short depending on how much you want to plant. The end part, when you bring yourself out of this relaxed state, is usually rather short. Let's take an example all the way through the three parts, and then we will look at other patterns that you can substitute or that you may want to make up for yourself. This image making is best done in a chair or on a bed or even on the floor. For safety's sake it should never be used when driving a car.

This is an example of an image that I use for total acceptance of myself. You can image yourself through these steps or the following could be read into your tape recorder and then listened to slowly.

I get myself into my chair or bed and unfasten any article of clothing that binds (like a belt or shoes). Then I relax in my special place with my feet and arms uncrossed because the circulation tends to stop when anything is crossed. As I get comfortable in my special place I open my mouth about a quarter of an inch, and now I begin the process, slowly closing my eyes so the energy does not flow out through them. I take a breath of air through my nose and slowly blow it out through my mouth. I try to get all the air out of my lungs by pushing the last part out (slight pause) I do this again through the nose and slowly push it out through the open mouth (slight pause). The next time when I take in a breath of air I hold it for second before blowing it all out remembering to push at the end so all the breath gets out (slight pause). I do this a fourth time (slight pause). I may notice that my body is starting to slow down and relax.

Next I focus on my head to see if there is any tightness around the ears or jaws and as I continue my slow breathing I blow out any of this tightness in my head and feel it relaxing. I next consider my neck and shoulders to see if there is any tightness in that area and slowly blow out that discomfort (pause). Still breathing slowly, I focus on my upper arms and check for any tightness there, next on my elbows, lower arms, wrists, and hands (pause). I slowly breathe out this tightness and let these parts of my body relax. Now I focus on my chest and let it relax, breathing out any tightness that I feel (pause). As I continue breathing slowly I focus on my stomach and check for any discomfort and slowly breathe out through my mouth (pause). Next I focus on my lower abdomen and look for any tightness and slowly relax and breathe out that tightness through the mouth(pause). Now I take several breaths of air and let my upper body relax. Then I can focus on my thighs and see if there is any discomfort and slowly blow that discomfort out through my mouth (pause). Next I focus on my knees and calves and look for any tightness and slowly breathe that out through my mouth (pause). I focus on my ankles and feet and look for anything that makes them uncomfortable and breathe that out through my mouth letting my entire body relax. Then I focus on my spine and let it completely relax, breathing out any tightness (pause). Last of all I let my mind go completely blank. I let go of any worries and breathe them out (pause). Now my whole body is relaxing (pause).

Next I picture myself coming to ten steps by a garden. Next to the steps is a handrail that I can hold onto if I need it. Starting on the top of the ten steps, I can feel my body relaxing. As I step down to the ninth step, I feel my body relaxing a little more. I step down to the eighth step and slowly breathe in and out, relaxing a little more. As I go down to the seventh and sixth step my body relaxes even more (pause). As I hold the rail and go to the fifth step again my body relaxes still more. Then onto the fourth and the third step breathing slowly and allowing my body to relax completely. Next the second step and finally the first, until I step out into the garden feeling very relaxed.

As I slowly walk out into the garden, I listen to the sounds as my feet touch the path and I relax. The smells of the fresh air are wonderful as it fills my lungs. The faint smells of flowers and damp grass relax me more (pause). I come upon a double wicker chair with large comfortable pillows and slowly sit down in the softness of the pillows. As I sit there I can hear a small brook off in the distance running happily over some rocks (pause). Off in the distance I see some gently rolling hills and everything seems to fit in the picture. As I sit in my special place I feel very comfortable and at home (pause). I just sit quietly and breathe slowly, letting my entire body relax.

As I am sitting there quietly, I see a figure slowly approaching me from the path. As the figure gets closer to me I see that it is God. He smiles at me and I smile back. He comes up and sits down next to me in the chair and takes my hand (pause). The two of us just sit quietly, and I can feel the acceptance in God's hand (pause). I don't have to tell God my problems since God already knows. The two of us just sit there quietly looking at nature (pause). I can feel the total acceptance. As we are sitting there looking at the garden a bumblebee comes up and slowly does a dance among the flowers. The two of us watch the dance (pause). All of a sudden another bumblebee comes into the area and a game of tag takes place between the two bees. We laugh together as we watch the two bees (pause). After that the two of us just observe nature and how everything fits in the picture (pause). Then God slowly gets up and gives my hand a squeeze, reassuring me that I can have God back any time that I want. After that, God walks a distance away. He turns and gives me a wave and a smile, which I return. Meanwhile, I am sitting quietly in the garden breathing slowly and observing each of my senses, being aware of what I feel. Maybe I feel the sunshine on my head or soft breaths on my arms or body. These let me know that I belong (pause). I can continue to be here as long as I wish.

Now it is time to leave. I take a deep breath and can feel the energy coming back into my arms and legs. Next I can feel my whole body coming back. Everything speeds up, including the beating of my heart . Now I move my fingers and toes and slowly move my hands and feet. Then I slowly open my eyes and I am back in my surroundings.

To restate the three parts: relaxation is the beginning. If you want the short form, just do the breathing part. The body relaxation and the steps going down into the garden enable the image to go deeper into one's subconscious.

The middle part is the image of the garden with God. I will give some other options on this part in the next chapter.

The last part is returning to reality and can be done by counting to four or five as you breathe energy back into the body. A word of caution: don't get up suddenly since you might be weak, and you could fall if your movement is too quick. Move slowly.

The Garden of Images

Here are some images that can be used in the middle part of the imagination exercise. The relaxation part is always done before these images.

An Image for Reducing Anxiety

As you are breathing, slowly imagine sitting some place in nature that is very safe, by yourself. Watch a small cloud coming into the sky above you (pause). As the cloud slowly moves overhead it gradually comes to a stop, just above your chair. Pick up an imaginary basket next to your chair and place some of the anxiety you are feeling about your particular situation in the basket. Hook the basket to a part of the cloud, and watch the cloud slowly rise back into the sky and drift off to the horizon (pause). Breathe easily and let your body relax as the anxiety drifts away (pause). After a period of time slowly bring yourself back to reality.

Another Image for Reducing Anxiety

As you are breathing deeply, imagine yourself sitting on a very quiet beach in your special chair. Focus on any sounds or smells that your senses pick up on the beach as you relax in your special chair (pause). Maybe you hear birds along the beach, or you can feel the warm sand as it runs through your fingers. Pick up the small boat next to the chair, and try to intensify the feeling of hurt about your particular situation (pause). Now take some of this feeling and put it into the boat and place the boat into the water. Watch the waves slowly take the boat out into the water (pause). Breathe easily as the boat gets farther away until it disappears into the horizon (pause). Now the anxiety should be less than you previously experienced. This exercise can be done more than once. Now gradually bring yourself back to reality.

Both of the above exercises can be done with regard to any emotion, including anger.

An Image for Freeing the Spirit

As you are breathing deeply and resting in your favorite chair, imagine sitting in a meadow (pause). See yourself as a small child running through the meadow with a beautifully colored kite (pause). Feel the breeze on your body as you run and enjoy the complete openness (pause). Come to a stop as your kite rises into the blue sky and dances among the clouds (pause). It is free to go in whatever direction it chooses. The richness of the colors of the kite blends with the sky (pause). You laugh as a bird flies over and plays with the kite. You don't have a worry in the world (pause). Breathe slowly in and out as you enjoy this picture. After a time bring yourself back to reality.

Relaxing the Whole Body

Imagine yourself sitting by a brook breathing slowly as you relax your entire body (pause). Picture yourself to be about five years old. Sitting next to you is a bucket of warm honey. You pick up the bucket and slowly pour the honey over your head (pause). As the honey oozes down over your head, it feels very warm and comfortable (pause). As the honey inches down over your shoulders and entire body, all your aches and pains disappear (pause). Magically, after the honey flows over your entire body down to your feet, it runs back into the bucket and your body is completely relaxed (pause). Sit there for a time and feel this complete relaxation (pause). Then slowly bring yourself back to reality.

Calming the Spirit or the Mind

Breathe deeply several times while in your special place as you walk around a corner up to a quiet pond (pause). As you stand by the pond notice any colors in the area and how wonderfully peaceful the image is (pause). Slowly walk into the pond and sit down with the waters up to your shoulders. Notice how warm and peaceful the water is with your body. Allow the peaceful quiet to enter every part of your body and mind (pause). Just remain quiet and still as the water of the pond in nature heals you (pause). After a time bring yourself back to reality.

Healing a Part of the Mind

After doing your breathing exercise, image sitting in nature in your special place (pause). As you do this, picture yourself possessing a toy vacuum cleaner with large colorful wheels. Imagine yourself running this vacuum cleaner up and down and around the different parts of the mind, cleaning up any dust that represents the pain from your hurtful situation (pause). Get into all the different corners and areas that need cleaning and take as much time as you need (pause). After doing this for a while, imagine cleaning out the bag of the vacuum cleaner, and holding it up in the wind and watching the dust blow away (pause). Now slowly bring yourself back to reality. This can be done as many times as you need, and each time the hurt will lessen.

Healing a Part of the Body

After the body is relaxed, picture yourself in your special place (pause). Slowly take a breath of sunlight into your lungs. Feel the warmth and healing that takes place in this area. Now imagine this warmth slowly moving to the part of the body that is giving you trouble (pause). Slowly allow this warmth to permeate the troublesome area (pause). Then breathe out any discomfort in the form of a gray smoke (pause). Do this as many times as you need to heal this area (pause). Now slowly bring yourself back to reality.

Building a Healthy Boundary Around Your Personality

Again, relaxing the body by your breathing exercise, imagine yourself walking into a beautiful flower garden and taking a seat near the middle (pause). Look around the garden and see all the beautiful flowers of different colors and shapes, and see how they all belong there (pause). Around the edge of the garden is a white picket fence with a gate at one end (pause). Be aware of how safe you feel in the garden with the fence around you (pause). Just sit there and enjoy the garden (pause). After a time, walk over to the edge of the garden and look out over the picket fence (pause). Just walk around in your garden and enjoy the different areas, since it is your garden (pause). Walk over to the gate where you can go out, if you wish, or just stay in the garden (pause). Maybe someone comes to the gate and you allow him or her to come in for a time. Then let that person go out when you wish. All the time you feel very comfortable in your garden, your safe place (pause). After you do this for a time, begin to energize yourself by inhaling deeply several times. The more you do this exercise, the stronger the boundaries for your personality will become.

Healing the Memory of the Hurt

Allow your body to relax using your breathing exercise, and imagine sitting on a beach where the tide slowly goes in and out (pause). Listen to any sounds, which could be the waves pounding against the shore or birds singing along the beach (pause). Sit down by the edge with your feet in the water, and feel the gentleness as the warm water washes over your feet (pause). Each time the water washes over your feet feel the hurt slowly being washed out of your body (pause). Your entire body starts to relax more and more (pause). After doing this for a comfortable period of time, energize your body by doing your breathing exercise.

Healing Acceptance of Self

Do your breathing exercise to relax the body, then imagine sitting on a double seat in a quiet meadow. As your body and mind settle down, notice all the things in nature that your five senses pick up (pause). You may smell the wet grass or wild flowers. You may notice sounds of the wind, or birds, or even leaves blowing in the distance (pause). Perhaps you will feel the warmth of the sun or the cool of the air on your body, along with any other feeling that your senses pick up. All that time your body is relaxing more and more (pause). Off in the distance a figure walks into the picture who you realize is God. He walks up to you and sits down next to you and takes your hand and holds it. Notice the warmth that comes into your hand. Slowly the warmth goes up your arm into your entire body (pause). Calmness spreads through your entire body, and the two of you just observe nature (pause). Occasionally God smiles. You don't have to explain anything about your situation, since God already knows. You feel quietness over your whole being as the two of you relax and enjoy nature (pause). After a time, God gets up and slowly walks away with a smile and a wave. You do not worry, since you can call him back whenever you wish (pause). You continue to sit and enjoy nature, breathing slowly (pause). After a time, do the breathing exercise to put energy back into your body and open your eyes. Then spend some time just relaxing in your chair.

These are some of the images that you can use, but many people choose to make their own images. Next we will look at some ways to help you do this.

Building Your Own Images

Some people have difficulty imaging at first, while others find it easy. If you have difficulty, here are some suggestions that may help you. First just look out the window at the scene outside for a few minutes, then close our eyes and try to picture what you saw. Sam liked to remember when he was fishing and later frying the fish. He would use all his senses to remember what happens in this scene. He could even remember the sounds of the fish frying. So use any of your senses, visual, sound, or smell, or even body positions, since all our senses are connected. If you are verbal, just describe what you saw to your mind. After a time this will become easier.

If you have no trouble imagining, then use metaphors like warm honey pouring over your body, or a cool breeze on your face, or your body bathed in warm sunlight or immersed in running water. Use any image that relaxes you. Just by using your imagination you build trust in yourself over a period of time, which will help you with your choices. As you feed the mind true statements that are connected, your intuition is free to accept healing statements. As the body relaxes more, you can just let go. This allows the intuition of the mind to focus more deeply on the healing image. If you are recording the imaging exercise on tape, changing the tone of your voice helps.

With the breathing exercise, it is very important that the out-breathing be done, since this helps the body relax

and quiet down. Medical people call this the parasympa-
thetic nervous system and the vagus nerve. This helps us to
slow down and relax. If you connect statements and behav-
iors this helps when you are in the situation. As I breathe
deeply my whole body relaxes. If I get tense while shopping,
for example, I can breathe deeply and my body will relax.

Alice found that if she made choices in her relaxation
exercises, her mind and body relaxed more. It helped her if
she stated to herself that she could relax her right arm and
then her right leg, rather than relaxing both arms at the same
time. Jeanne Achterberg talks about cross-sensing that helps
with imaging. She describes how you can "see" the sounds
around you, or "hear" the colors. The simpler the image, the
more powerful it is. Many of us are taught that the more
effort we put into something, the better the result. This is not
always true in the case of imaging. Better results can be
achieved if you practice imaging early in the morning or late
at night, since those are the times we pass from sleep to being
awake, from consciousness to unconsciousness.

In counseling we have a technique called *reframing*. For
example, you might continue to replay some hurt in a behavior in your mind. What if you changed the pattern to a more
correct or healthier behavior? Then, when you thought of
the hurtful behavior, instead of tightening up you could tell
yourself, "I am relaxing and my whole body is letting go."
Change will happen with this technique. Since emotions are
connected to images, change does take place in a very safe
way over a period of time. You may be surprised at the speed
of the change you experience when using these techniques.

Two-Minute Vacations

Sometimes we don't have an hour, or even a half an hour, to plant these images in the mind, and we have to make do with several minutes. The following is an exercise that I do many times during the day. I have taught it to many people who seem to enjoy its benefits—especially for relaxing. If you are at home or in an office, just take three or four deep breaths, slowly blowing them out through your mouth. Than do one of the following images, or build your own.

Just look out a window and let the picture imprint on your mind as you relax. After you do this for several minutes, breathe energy back into your body and come back to reality.

After doing the breathing exercise look at a picture in a magazine or a photograph and imagine yourself in that location just observing nature. Again, bring yourself back to reality after several minutes.

Sit on a step by your home and enjoy the smell of fresh air, or any other pleasant smells that you pick up with your senses.

If you are sitting in the kitchen, imagine the fresh smells of something baked, like homemade bread, or the aromas of a favorite meal.

Imagine sitting by a stream, or some other source of running water, and listening to the sounds of the water as you relax.

Watch a bird overhead as it slowly makes circles in the sky and feel the freedom of the bird.

Watch some animal or even an ant as it makes it way through the yard or area of nature where you are sitting.

Listen to the sounds of water as it goes over a waterfall, or as it trickles down a small creek.

Feel the water run over your head or body as you take a shower, and feel your body relaxing.

Imagine yourself someplace where you were on vacation, and put yourself into that scene as you relax and enjoy yourself.

Remember when someone said something nice to you and how pleased you were when you heard him or her say it.

Remember how you felt when your pet looked at you with eyes of total acceptance, or how good it feels when you rub your pet.

Look at a picture on a calendar and imagine that you are in that picture.

Feel the pleasure when you imagine being with your closest friend, or in your most special place.

Imagine how it feels when you are listening to a favorite piece of music and how it relaxes your senses.

You can add any image that you are comfortable with, but always start with breathing slowly and then move into the image, finally bringing yourself back. Do not do this while driving a car since altered reality could cause an accident. This two-minute vacation works well when you use any of the senses. Each of us has one sense that we tend to favor, but the other four senses can be brought into play with practice. Relaxing the body and mind allows healthy images to come into the mind, which helps us to heal.

Back to the Garden

The Bible tells us that we all came originally from a garden, and that it was a perfect place. Using the imagination with deep relaxation, or the two-minute vacation, gives us a chance to look at some of the aspects of the garden.

What if we built a wall around our garden? A wall can be used to isolate us from others, or to give us a safe place to heal. All the people I have been talking about used it for a time to heal, but many became trapped within their own wall. Hank built his wall so high that he became emotionally trapped behind it. Sam used his wall as a weapon against others so he would not have to look at himself. Alice sat on hers so she could judge those around her. There is no question that each of these people was wounded by a situation, but at some place they stopped growing. If any of these people started to take a rock off their wall and place it by a stream in the garden, what could they learn?

The rock could teach them that life has a certain permanence about it, and that life goes on outside the wall. There is nature with all its beauty and its growth. But, like the rock that is hard, life is sometimes hard for all of us. If we remain behind the wall too long we get bored. Making a gate in the wall allows us to go out into nature and into the world, and begin to grow again. If you break a bone in your body, you need to take time to heal. But at some point, you have to put pressure on it again to move on in life. If staying in the garden causes you boredom or aimlessness, it may be time to reconnect to others. There is something about connecting with nature that helps the soul heal faster. Maybe it gives you a means to establish a spirituality that is well grounded.

An interesting quality of the stone is its strength. By sitting quietly, you can listen to the messages that come from this stone. You are doing two things. One, you are slowly lowering the wall to a level where you can look out and still be safe. Two, by taking the strength of the stone and the images that you have worked with you can slowly reach out and grow. Walls and stones can offer many metaphors about your life.

Sally and John stayed in the garden so long that they became bored. Children who sit around most of the time are bored and lack the enrichment that play provides. As these people started to introduce play into their lives, beginning in the garden, growth occurred and the boredom decreased. When was the last time you played in a safe way? Notice, I said in a safe way. The reason I say this is because after discussing play with one of the women, she put on a large yellow hat and went down to the local bar.

Just as I stated that life is a journey, so we have to come out of the garden and take some safe steps to connect—with nature first and then with others. There is a state park near where I live, and several times a week the ranger gives guided walks through the woods with a small group. Look around your area and see what is going on that is also safe. As you allow yourself to become intimate with the things around you, you will become enchanted with everyday life. Thomas Moore's book, *The Re-Enchantment of Everyday Life,* published by Harper in 1997, can help you with this.

Moving Out of the Garden

When the first part of your work is completed, and you have built a solid foundation from which to go forth, it is time for you to share some of your growth with others, as you might share some beautiful flowers you had grown.

Any time we try something new it is scary at first, like trying to ride a bicycle for the first time. At first we are not so sure of our moves, but after a short time it becomes easier. As we watch others who are successful, it makes our experience a little easier. My recommendation is to first join a safe group and hang around the edges to see how others function. Look in the paper or watch TV for groups that you may be interested in joining. Nature groups, walking expeditions, or public lectures are nice places to start. Or you might go to the store and engage a clerk in a conversation about some particular article.

Try watching how others interact in the mall or a restaurant. One of the people that I worked with agreed to meet a friend at a local restaurant. She was nervous and got there early, but the friend never did show up because she had had car trouble. When she said that the waiter kept asking her if he could help her, I asked her, jokingly, if she had the tablecloth over her head, since he was so insistent on helping her. We laughed about the situation, and looked for options that she could do so she would not feel as though she stood out. We came up with the idea of taking a newspaper or a book and simply ordering a cup of coffee or tea until the friend showed up. Several people said that they sometimes would go to a movie in the afternoon and were surprised at how many single people also came in to watch the movie.

Sally stated that she was trying to remove two words from her conversation with others—*always* and *never*. She felt that in her previous relationships she got into trouble whenever she used these two words. When she used them she felt that she boxed the other person in and did not leave room for another option. Words like *sometimes* or *maybe* provide the freedom to consider more than one choice.

Sam noticed that there were lots of "shoulds" and "oughts" in his life, which provided a heavily parental message. Whenever someone said something to him using these words, his hair stood up on the back of his neck. Sam practiced giving his own opinion in groups. If others disagreed, he would tell himself that it was okay to have another opinion. Each time he would listen to the statement and evaluate it and see if he agreed with part of it. As his confidence grew, he found that it was easier for him to express his opinion.

Leaving the Garden Reflects Leaving Home Again

The Early Years

You started your life in a condition where all your needs were met. That is when you were in your mother's womb. You had complete oneness with your mother. It was a perfect environment. During that period of oneness with your mother, you had closeness and complete dependence; it was warm and all your needs were met. As you grew in the womb, the space became more confining; then eventually you were born. Being born meant the beginning of a certain separateness, an independence of being—though you were still entirely dependent upon your mother. Birth meant leaving the warmth of your mother's womb and entering the colder world outside, where your needs were not always met.

With birth you were beginning the process of leaving home. By learning to deal with the process of life, a person grows. That growth involves dealing with the conflict over making choices between polarities—oneness and separateness. The first step in the physical process is when you are born. You did not have too much choice at that time, but as you matured the process forced more choices on you. But let's continue with this journey which is leaving home.

In the first months of life, you learned two things: molding and bridging. You practiced molding when your mother held you and you fitted snugly in her arms. You adapted. Even at that early stage you had the gift, in a way, of making your mother feel confident as a mother as she held you and fed you. Your earlier oneness with her was being reestablished. In addition to molding, in those early months, you were also learning how to bridge. Bridging occurred when you curved your back and pushed with your feet; you were working for some separateness, or some distancing, from your mother.

As you grew you started to take some risks. Learning to walk, you let go of your mother's knee and tried to move on your own, but always with an eye to that supporting knee. It was as though you wanted some separateness, yet did not want to give up the oneness with mother just yet. Once again, your "giftedness" stepped in. During this time you found that trusting your father, or some other male adult friend of your mother could be deliciously exciting. Say, your mother was going out for the afternoon, leaving you with your father or a male friend. That was a time to bend the rules or to forget about them completely. Then, when your mother returned, she found you overly tired or even upset, but even so, you had had a good time.

Babies at this stage can only deal with a little separateness. As the months passed you ventured farther from your mother's side: you crept through a doorway into the next room, where you could no longer see her. To get her attention you had to call out or cry, to bring her nearer. At the age of about sixteen months you developed an ability to imagine; that's the way you began expanding your world, the way you began "leaving home."

At the age of two you took another big step. That's the age referred to as the "terrible two's." It's a kind of second birth, of psychological awakening. At about that age you began setting boundaries between yourself and the outer world. For example, let's say you were standing on a chair holding a glass of milk. Though one of your parents had said, "Don't you dare spill your milk," you deliberately poured it on the floor. At age two you felt like the king of the mountain. The house was your realm for a year or so. In reality you were dealing with your oneness and establishing how much of the world is you, and how much of it is outside of you. It was a difficult time for you, as well as for your parents, but again, you handled the situation with your own giftedness. Step by step you launched the process of leaving home by setting your own boundaries on an emotional and physical level.

As you continued to grow, you began to take further risks. Probably you got to stay overnight at your grandmother's, or with a friend. Watching your mother pack your little bag for the big event was exciting, and your parents' encouragement helped, too. That visit, and others like it, gave you more experience of separateness, of leaving home. Sam actually remembers going to his grandmother's house for the first time.

School and Adolescence

Next, it was off to school. Thanks to the loving care of your parents—and teachers as well—you accomplished this step. At school you expanded your social skills and learned new things, among them that it's easier to leave home if you have a group of friends. You learned it was pleasant being down the street, away from home, playing with friends. You felt reassured, though: home wasn't far away. You wanted some separateness, but not too much! Thus you continued through childhood.

In the adolescent years you were so busy separating that at times you did not know where you came from. Those years were difficult for you, as well as for your parents. Your striving for separateness may have been expressed in one of three different ways. After an argument with your parents, you may have run out of the house, with all your energy directed *away* from the house. Or you may have backed out of the house, with all your energy directed *toward* the house. These two ways left much unfinished in the process of leaving home. In the third way, you left the house *side-ways*; that is, you did not cut your roots or your connection to home, but on leaving you knew the way you wanted to go. Adolescents go through an especially difficult period as the time for leaving home physically and emotionally comes ever nearer. Mary remembers running out of the house on many occasions during this period of her life.

In your late teens you were leaving the world of youth and stepping into the adult world. Many of your childhood needs or desires were forever gone: instant pleasure, maximum security, minimum responsibility, having things go your way. It was a time when you were good at relating to your parents, when your motivations were plainly evident, and when you learned to communicate in a vertical fashion.

Adulthood

In the adult world, you quickly learn that instant pleasure is not the norm; the norm is sacrifice. Adults have to give in many times. As for maximum security, in the adult world you have to take certain risks in order to grow. This applies to work, to education, and to one's most personal, intimate affairs. Responsibility is based upon giving, receiving, and taking—depending upon the situation. Where communication was vertical during the youthful years, now it is horizontal. You are now communicating adult to adult, not child to adult. That puts you on a different level, even with your own parents, who still continue seeing you, perhaps, more as a child than as a young adult.

Another aspect of your growing separateness might be on the spiritual level. You may have thrown away many of the values your parents tried to instill in you. Now you strive for your own set of values. That takes time and effort, but having a set of values does give direction to your life. The child part of you tends to avoid having anything to do with the spiritual part since it's easier not to assume responsibility. Your position in the adult world stems from good adult-to-adult relationships, and that involves internalizing your values. John did little to set up his own values; however, he disliked the values of other adults.

As you leave home physically, life becomes more complex. You may have used stepping stones to get there: going away to college, entering the military, perhaps getting married. That is all right, assuming you *complete* the process of leaving home.

When you leave home your role as an adult changes. In relationship to your parents, you are an adult the same as they are. Their role changes, too. They continue to love you and may be willing to help on occasion, but their responsibility for you is over. Psychologists say that a person is a provisional adult until about age thirty. Parents, meanwhile, gradually let go of the "shoulds" and "oughts" and move into a nurturing position of love, which for most lasts the rest of their lives.

For the majority of us, home becomes a condition at this time, more than anything else. We leave the physical home where we grew up, but what we learned there helps to start our new life "out there." Home and family, and the emotions these arouse, provide a type of support system that we always have with us.

Learning to Love

Now our task in adulthood is to fully develop our capacity for love. This is done in three areas. First, we develop our conscious life with respect to intelligence, will, memory, senses, imagination, and physical health. Second, we need to look at our inner being to discover the many powers of our unconscious which give direction to our lives. And third, we must develop our sense of community—our ability to relate to others. These three areas take a lifetime to complete; all the while, our parents are ahead of us in this journey of life. We can learn from their experience. It's like a group of people traveling to a particular place. The first person may hit certain potholes on the trip, then warn the other travelers of these road conditions. We profit from others' experience, particularly that of our parents. Parents pass the kinship bond on to their children, who in turn pass it on to their own children. It is sad when families fail to attain this connectedness by not sharing their experiences.

So you learn to love in your life. That love must be brought into proper balance and tension with the love of self, love of neighbor, and love of God. Parents and grandparents are part of this system. This does not mean that you always approve of their behavior or their advice, or that they approve of yours. But the basic line is that you and they care for one another. Sally always hated herself, so she had a poor basis on which to build love of neighbor and love of God.

Honing In

As we grow older in life, so do our parents, and eventually, of course, they die. When the first parent dies, you feel as if you have lost a part of yourself. Although there is a radical change in your relationship to home, the fact that one of your parents is still there makes you feel you can, if things get really bad, still go home. When that parent dies, you realize that you are really alone. The only home remaining for you is your own and you begin to hone in on it. You become ever more aware of what your parents gave you, sacrificed for you, and you may now regret not having expressed your gratitude more while they were alive.

Gratitude can be shown to our parents in a number of patterns. Caring, flexibility, and balance are three patterns that help the family to continue to grow. *Balance* here means the give-and-take that is necessary for happy, lasting relationships. In adulthood there is a certain degree of giving that one never gets back. The word for this used to be *sacrifice*. When both sides—the parents and their grown-up children—work from a model of caring, flexibility, and balance, both sides seem to grow in a healthier pattern. Gratitude, then, can work both ways: from adult children to parents, and from parents to adult children.

As I've tried to explain, leaving home is a process and there are many steps involved. Most of us handle the process well, but we have to remember that it is a human process and that there are difficulties at times. I believe that a sense of humor always helps in times of transition, as the following story illustrates.

A son was bringing his ninety-eight-year-old mother to church one day in the fall. She was only five feet tall and weighed about ninety pounds; the son was over six feet tall. Her head was covered with a black shawl. She loudly insisted on going to the front row. Seated there, she kept pulling her shawl close because of the cold. During the sermon it grew colder, yet the homilist kept talking and talking. Finally the woman said, in a loud voice, "It's cold in here. Why don't they turn up the heat?" The congregation tittered; the homilist's face grew red, but he kept talking; the son tried to hush his mother. The sermon continued. At long last the mother loudly asked her son: "Why is he talking so long?" Needless to say, the sermon abruptly ended, and the people in the pews were trying to stifle their laughter. The son in this story was Hank.

Parents sometimes embarrass their children, but then the children have often embarrassed their parents. In either case, a sense of humor helps.

Something Is Still Missing

So what happened to Mary, John, Alice, Sam, and Sally, with their hurts, and how did they process past these situations? Most of them isolated themselves by one means or another from the pain they were experiencing. You may do the same thing with your own hurts. However, this may result in the tendency to isolate yourself not only from your pain and hurts, but from your joys as well, so that very little growth takes place in your system or theirs. Most people tend not to have intimacy or love with someone else when they don't experience it with themselves, because of a lack of trust. The first part of this book was meant to help us rediscover the goodness, peace, and wellness in ourselves. When we show compassion for ourselves, we often start to show compassion for others.

We do this by opening our hearts and starting to love ourselves. When you tell your story to another person, and that person does not judge what you are saying, this occurs. The person who just listens without judgment creates the bond of trust which then encourages us to so reach out to others. This healing is the process of becoming whole. In my lectures I always explain that wholeness and holiness come from the same Greek word that means to heal. So when John, Alice, Sam, and the others learned to open their emotional hearts, healing took place not only on a physical, but also on a spiritual level. As they worked on their emotional hurts, spiritual healing began to take place.

If they did not work on their healing process, more isolation and aloneness resulted. The color left their lives and few experienced the joys of life. Some drank too much, or ate too much, or worked too much or, like some of us, channel surfed too much. We use whatever technique helps us to avoid pain or looking at a situation that needs change. Pain is only an agent telling us that something needs to change or be looked at. Many of us want a cure handed to us, because then we don't have to change. But pain and hurt can be the opening that gives us direction toward wholeness and holiness.

When I worked in high schools, many young people wanted to be popular and connected to others but did not know how. Sometimes they turned to unhealthy ways and joined gangs where they ended up fighting anyone who was different from those in their group. They were really looking for wholeness and a sense of belonging.

My purpose in the earlier chapters of the book was to help build a healthy foundation for these young people and you, my readers, using meditation, imagery, self-hypnosis, and similar techniques. All of us experience aloneness at times. This is not the same as loneness. Aloneness is like being in the house or a room by yourself. To change this all you have to do is leave and go where other people are. Loneness is like being in a room and looking out the windows, and the windows become mirrors so that all you see is yourself. Some of this can be resolved by going out with other people. If this is existential loneness, then there is not much you can do about it. There is always a space between you and others, since you are a separate being. This is only resolved when you return to God. But this type of loneness passes after a time.

As Sam and the rest learned to be close to others, they also learned to be more vulnerable. This implies some trust and being able to risk. Clifton and Nelson in their book, *Soar with Your Strengths*, say there are two kinds of risks. One is called situational risk, as where you and your friends are in the middle of a storm and everyone pulls together. This can cause friendships that last a long time. The second kind of shared risk is when you and a partner purchase a home, or share some intimate information between the two of you. Here trust develops quickly, if both prove trustworthy. Young people can especially be hurt in this area since their boundaries are not as well established as those of older adults.

So what do you do when the trust breaks? I retreat into my head, and then my mind becomes somewhat cold and I often end up angry. If I move into my heart, however, I tend have more compassion and am warmer to others and myself. When you first leave the garden, if you leave too quickly and find you are outside the fence, it is scary. As the fence is your safe boundary, so all relationships need boundaries. If I continue to choose people that are hanging on to unresolved issues, I can get hurt, or allow them to hurt me, while I blame them. Look at your patterns from the past and be aware of how you related to people. Grow from your mistakes, for we all make them. As you slowly open your heart, growth will begin like a new spring.

As these people, and you, build a foundation and proceed to come out of the garden, healing takes place. One of the steps, after telling your story, is awareness. Dean Ornish, M.D., in his book, *Love and Survival,* tells us that our teachers in life come in many forms; we can learn from reading books, or from being in groups. He suggests we try whatever will work best for us. He speaks about soft spots where we share feelings that open our hearts, but sometimes we end up getting hurt by the person we opened up to. Dr. Ornish cautions that we should then try someone else who is not judgmental, as a judgmental response causes us to pull back and close up. He notes that when we are accepted in sharing our feelings, then we feel able to share even more openly.

Alice and the others started to share feelings like: I feel happy; I feel good; I feel alone (worried, anxious, angry, and the like). As a result, their hearts began to open and intimacy started to take place. Each found that his or her feelings were true. As they disclosed more of their feelings, they started to acknowledge the feelings of others. But they also found that it is all right to have a wall around your heart sometimes, and that you don't have to disclose everything all the time.

Just as all of us have moments when we experience difficulty dealing with our loneness, caring for others can help us. As Alice and the others found, the more they were connected with others, the healthier they became. But each of these people had to take time to quiet the mind and body so they could experience peace and happy moments. By using awareness, whether in meditation or by some other form, each was able to enjoy the senses more fully. As they developed their inner peace, they were able to have healthier relationships. Also, they tried to surround themselves with people that were less angry and more compassionate, thus giving themselves more time to open their hearts.

So what do I do to increase my awareness so compassion can grow? Try sitting down in a woods, by a lake, or in a meadow, to just observe nature. Sometimes I just lie on my bed with my eyes closed and reflect on some peaceful or happy event. I've even sat quietly in a mall and watched people passing by. The key is never judging, just observing, for judging closes the door to the heart. Going out is part of the healing situation, but go slowly and take risks that are safe and small. Being aware—awareness—is just one of the safe things to do as you begin to go out.

Hurt Partners in a Marriage

What happens when a person experiences a deep hurt, as Sam did, in a broken marriage? What happens when a trauma situation, like being in a war, or childhood abuse, or losing a child to death, puts a lot of strain on a relationship? What Sam did showed that he felt polarized and alienated from his partner by the way he grieved. Men and women grieve in different ways. Women are prone to talk, while men keep things to themselves. In Sam's case, he had persistent re-experiencing of the trauma: intrusive thoughts, nightmares, and flashbacks. You may experience different patterns.

Some of us use avoidance, by numbing ourselves into detachment. I know that I can use overeating for this purpose. These patterns usually end up in isolation when we try to soothe ourselves by drinking or using drugs. The other side of this is when we are in a state of constant alarm. The result either way is damage to the relationship, which slowly gets worse. All of these emotions are covered by depression or shame.

I would suggest couple therapy, so that the bond between the couple could get stronger and both parties could understand the trauma. But many times one party leaves the relationship, when with proper counseling the relationship could have become a stronger and safer place, and numbing would no longer have been needed. In such scenarios, the remaining partner loses the chance to express his or her hurts, fears, and anxiety. It is important for all of us to have a safe place to process our hurts so our fears do not block the path to more information.

When you are in a relationship and cannot handle a situation, it is well to seek help from a professional counselor and ask if he or she is trained in trauma therapy. Difficult relationships can add to previous problems experienced by one or both partners, and that need help.

What patterns do I use to handle my hurts?

The Language of Love

    As these people, on their journey back to wholeness, moved out of the garden, they began to have feelings of love for some other person. Here they might have difficulty learning a new language, a new way of relating to the other person. I call this the language of love and it is expressed in different ways. The first is visual and Mary was quite comfortable with this. She liked cards, flowers, and little tokens of love from her special friend. The second way is verbal—words of affection and appreciation. Hank needed to hear that he was loved. Sam, also, needed this and would become mellow and relaxed when he heard words of love. The third way is through touch. Sally, Alice, and John were more comfortable with this form. Problems occur when individual needs are different in the same couple—one needing visual expressions of love, while the other wanted love expressed verbally or by touch. For example, Mary preferred visual expression and she chose a fellow who liked touch. He would sit with his arm around her as they watched television. She was frustrated because she got no visual signs of affection from him. She would see a picture hanging slightly crooked on the wall and would have to get up and straighten it. He just wanted to sit with her. Sally was strongly verbal and yet her guy was not. He couldn't understand why she was upset, for he had told her he loved her during the first weeks of their relationship. That, unfortunately, was fourteen months ago! Each person had to find his or her way of expressing love and each had to work to try to meet the other's needs.

Conflicting Desires

Even when Adam and Eve were in the garden, and all their needs were met, they became dissatisfied. They got into trouble and had to leave the garden. There are going to be times in your life when you are discontented. This is a condition of life. Take this example from our lives; each of us started out at home and left it. Some of us ran out of the house, and when we got into the street we never knew which way we were going, other than that we were running *from* the house. Others of us backed out of the house, yelling at the house, so that when we got into the street all of our energy was directed at the house, as if we were shooting at it with a gun blazing in each hand. In both of these examples, our energy was directed at the house. A few of us went out of the house side-ways, so when we got into the street we knew what direction we wanted to go and where the house was, if we needed support. Those of us that were hurt also made our way out, and some of us want to go back, which is not possible. We all want to go back to a perfect house. Just as God made it right for Adam and Eve, allowing his Son to open the gates of Paradise again, so we too can make our lives on earth right with our God again. But this takes time. To have conflicting desires is a normal part of life. We can't always tie everything up in a neat package.

How did I leave my home?

Values and Prayer

Each of the people that I worked with had to deal with their values at one time or another. This created a problem for them since it made them get in touch with their God. As I grew older, I came to understand the tremendous power of emotions and the benefits of controlling these emotions. Likewise, the people I worked with came to the realization that prayer, or turning to God, helped them with their decision making when emotions were involved. Whereas they all had desires, prayer helped support healthy decisions when emotions colored the situation.

Just as Sally, Alice, and John felt very disconnected from the world around them, they also felt disconnected from their God. Sam was not sure he wanted to believe in God since he felt that God mostly was someone who punished people. Most agreed to try prayer to see if this established some sort of balance in their lives. I don't know if it was faith or their surrender to God's will that moved them. Some, at times, confused prayer, and turning their situation over to God, with magic, or getting God to do what they wanted. Most just got tired of being sad and wanted this misery to pass, so they did something by turning it over to God. I do the same with hurtful situations that I want God to fix. Then, when God does not perform according to my expectations and I get angry, God says to me: "How can *I* fix it? *You* never really let it go." One of the ways we were all helped was to turn the situation over to God and watch how God handled it.

Another technique I shared with those I helped was to pray for the people that had hurt me. After a period of time my attitude and theirs started to change. Maybe that is an indication of hope, since there seems to be a harmony that comes back into our lives. I think this reaching out of someone to their God from the limits of their visibility is really hope. The problem that many have is that on the one hand there is anger, and on the other hand there is hope, and finding the answer is somewhere in between. This is called recovery or healing.

The Kansas Garden

When I lived in Kansas for a number of years, the agricultural department had an area on the edge of the city where people who lived in apartments could have a plot 20' by 30' for a garden. Most of the people around me knew a lot about planting and mulching the garden, and the plots were an earthworm's delight. Many evenings I visited with my neighbors and friends in this garden and they all seemed to have plans for their own garden plot. Along with this planning, we shared our knowledge of seeds, plants, and vegetables.

As I watched these experienced gardeners, I learned about boundaries and borders. I planted my eight tomato plants very early and we had a hard freeze, so the next day I got eight more plants, covered them with straw, and the following night it snowed. My wise neighbor gently advised me to wait ten days. Then I planted eight more plants. In the end they all grew, so I had enough tomatoes for everyone. Just like in counseling, I was not always sure what methods to use with the people. Some worked and others did not, but I did pray a lot for each of the people and their problems. I told them they got something extra when they came to my office. This was prayer!

One thing the garden taught me was not to be surprised when it took time for ideas to grow in people. In the garden I would end up sweaty, dirty, and doing some things that were not planned. This was similar to counseling people on their life problems, which left many of them feeling sweaty or even dirty, and doing new things that took them out of their comfort zones. This is when the redemption takes place. Just as in the garden my weeds were always a reminder that a lapse in vigilance had taken place, so these people had to be watchful that they did not fall back into former mind patterns. Working in the dirt led to the enjoyment of beautiful flowers and the sharing of fresh vegetables.

I encouraged those I was counseling to work with plants in nature, since this seemed to put some balance back into their lives. As they watched the butterflies and hummingbirds doing their dance among the flowers, they started to see some of the happy times in their lives. Getting involved with nature helped some of them with their redemption.

What idea would I like to grow in me?

How can I nurture this concept in my mind and heart?

Sunlight

Sunlight plays a very important role in our lives. There are two ways it affected the people that I worked with. First, sunlight allows us to see clearly what is going on. Also, much solar energy is stored in vegetables, corn, wheat, and other foods. But sunlight is much more than illumination and energy.

Isaac Newton held a prism up to the sun, which created a rainbow. If we break the sunlight into its parts, it's like the world. It's made up of diversity, complexity, and variety—in individuals and races. We take in information by using our senses of touch, smell, taste, and sight. As each of the people I work with takes in information around them they notice patterns and become more aware. With this awareness they build their stories and history based upon their experiences. Then they set up rules, laws, and what they believe is right and wrong, like a value system. From this they may make predictions about themselves and others.

When Isaac Newton took a second prism and let the rainbow shine through, the varieties of light became sunlight again. The first prism is like collecting information, while the second is like putting it back together, similar to wisdom. The first system is an open book while the second one is what to do with the information in the book. Most of these people spend much time with the first and need to spend more time with the second, putting things back together. Or at least trying to make some sense out of the matter collected, if possible. Alice, Sam, and Sally replayed the information and got a high out of being mad about what had happened to them. This way they could blame their present failures on the past, not on what they were doing in the present. But as they learned about nature and the different seasons, they could learn to let go and move on. Just as in nature, things die and a new season starts, so people can let the past die and, even though they feel sad about certain things, they can still move on. They can occasionally be sad or angry about things, but it does not have to control their present life. But to do this they have to substitute something in its place.

Source of Love

I was at a talk recently where the speaker kept mentioning "letting go and letting God." This sounded so easy, but most of the people that I work with are always trying to fix this, or do that, and most of their days are taken up with many activities. They have more and more things to do, and as a result they never seem to finish. I saw that they were always tired and discouraged and many times overloaded with work.

I encouraged them to take breaks, to just sit down sometimes and do nothing. As their bodies quieted down, they started to heal. If you watch a small child sit at a piano and play one note over and over, you'll notice that the time between the notes gets longer. This time is the healing time in our lives.

When my counselees took time to sit by themselves and invited God to sit with them, things began to happen. They did not have to explain anything to God since he already knew.

You, also, can give yourself the time and space to do the healing process. After sitting for a fixed time with God, you can get up and go on with life again. As with a child, little steps are always safer at first, so you do not fall. But take time to build the practice of sitting with God.

Little Glances

A nice habit to develop as you go about life is to take small glances at God with your imagination. When you are in a growth pattern it may be painful. If so, just glance at God, who is right beside you. This is a pattern that I helped my people to develop as they dealt with the feelings and memories of past hurts.

When they were busy mowing the lawn, cleaning the sink, doing laundry, feeding the kids, or even working on an assembly line, they just glanced at God who was beside them. This gave them added strength to continue with their work. This is an example of building a love relationship with God. Looking to God, in a sense, is like looking homeward, to our final home. These small glances allow our hearts to move closer to our friend—God. Such added strengths are always very helpful in life.

Images of God

Most of us know about God through the people that we were with when younger, or through what we have read. But what happened to you or to others who experienced a deep hurt when younger? Do you approach God by prayer or conversation? Is God male or female, a loving parent or critical, mean or trusting? Does God make you feel guilty or accepted? What did you learn from your parents, teachers, churches, or those in charge? My experience when I am hurt, or work with those that are hurting, is that it seems as though God is a "critical" parent and not a caring one. Many of those I have worked with did not want to think about God at all. Maybe it is me that is critical and uncaring. Perhaps I have developed an unhealthy pattern of holding others away from me, so I do not have to experience any feeling at all.

In working with a person who had had a terribly abusive parent, I gave this fellow a long caring fatherly hug at the end of each interview to replace what was missing when he was a child. As he slowly healed, he became more loving and accepting of himself.

So each of us will have to find new images of our God that are loving, accepting, and positive. One way that works for me when I don't have someone to share with, is to sit in a large old church and just look at a stained glass window that has a pleasant picture in it. For some reason the colors from the window seem to help me. Others have told me of listening to music, sitting in a garden, sitting in their home inhaling the aromas coming from the kitchen, or just going for a long walk in a park.

It's like God is always there, and we have to become quiet enough to listen to hear God. We just sit with God in a pleasant place. We lapse into silence, since God already knows what is going on.

What is my image of God?

How can I add more gentle views of God to help me?

Closing This Chapter of Life

As Sally, Sam, Alice, John, Mary, and Hank finished their counseling, each realized that this was only one chapter in their lives. They did not have to look at their future through a filter of their past experience. They put these memories away in a safe place in their mind and occasionally would take them out to look at whatever part of their past was starting to control their present life, and then put it back. By looking at their family, their fears, and their feelings, each realized that they could let go of the hurtful memories and continue to enjoy life. Some even had a particular time, such as in the morning, when they could have a good cry, letting their feelings out and then moving on. They found out that tears were okay. They found that they could love again and share with others. When they found that vengeance or stubbornness were a waste of time, they moved on to forgiveness of others and themselves.

An Artist and a Canvas

Pretend that you sneaked a preview of a large painting in process. Off in the distance the faint shades and hues were blended into the background and many were abstract and difficult to figure out. Most of the patterns, objects, trees, and people were like a distant memory. The artist painted with much emotion and was committed to the painting. You could tell that the artist really loved this work and painted areas of life (the bright colors) and areas of hurt (the muted colors). The love of the artist was bringing the plain canvas to life. The canvas is not complete, yet it is well to trust the artist. The canvas is your life with your good times and your bad times. The artist is God, and it's good to trust the Artist who loves you and who gives you the strength that you need for life. You are a work of art in process, and God, the Artist, is not finished with you yet. Each day the Artist adds to the canvas, sometimes lighting some dark area showing things we might rather not see, and other times using colors so rich and vibrant that we are filled with joy. Remember that God's love is always on your side. Just as God the Artist shows love in creation, the Artist does not rest until that love is reflected in all that the Artist, God, creates. Remember, you are God's creation.

Suggestions for Further Reading

Clifton, Donald Q. and Paula Nelson. *Soar with Your Strengths*. New York: Dell Publishing, 1995.

Lerner, Harriet Goldhor. *The Dance of Anger*. New York: Harper Trade, 1985.

McCullough, Michael. *To Forgive Is Human*. Westmont: Inter Varsity Press, 1997.

Meninger, William A. *The Process of Forgiveness*. New York: Continuum International, 1997.

Moore, Thomas. *The Re-Enchantment of Everyday Life*. New York: Harper Trade, 1997.

Ornish, Dean., M.D. *Love and Survival*. San Francisco: Harper Collins, 1999.

Peck, M. Scott. *The Road Less Traveled*. New York: Simon & Schuster, 1978.